T0198910

# Dare to Believe in the Man in the Red Suit

*Melissa K. Larsen*

*Illustrated by Dan Drewes*

AuthorHouse™
1663 Liberty Drive
Bloomington, IN 47403
www.authorhouse.com
Phone: 833-262-8899

Because of the dynamic nature of the Internet, any web addresses or links contained in this book may have changed
since publication and may no longer be valid. The views expressed in this work are solely those of the author and do
not necessarily reflect the views of the publisher, and the publisher hereby disclaims any responsibility for them.

Any people depicted in stock imagery provided by Getty Images are models,
and such images are being used for illustrative purposes only.
Certain stock imagery © Getty Images.

This book is printed on acid-free paper.

ISBN: 978-1-4490-4134-2 (sc)

Print information available on the last page.

Published by AuthorHouse  10/29/2020

authorHOUSE®

This book would not be possible without those who Dared to Believe. I would like to acknowledge those who have given me the support and love to write this; my husband Kurt, my father Daddio, my special friends Chris and Valerie, my family, my coaches Chris and Carlene, Drs' Rick, Steve and Allan and my very own Santa who came to my open house year after year. John, for his ability to bring the young and the young at heart, to believe in what the man in the red suit represents.

My deepest inspiration comes from the years I had with my mom. This is really her story, which she gave to all 8 of her children year after year, as well to all those who knew her. Being able to see her unconditional love in print is the biggest tribute I can ever imagine... Mom, I love you!

For the prayers and support of all the prayer partners I have met in the 24/7 adoration chapels, to each of you, thank you.

This book is dedicated to all those who believe and carry that belief in their hearts and are willing to share it with others.

Today more than ever each one of us needs to step up and proclaim what we dare to believe and pass it on.

This is a story which started centuries ago and continues to be a precious gift handed down from one person and generation to the next. Do we dare to believe and share?

Thank you for choosing this book. The beliefs you share with your child and your inner child will be a seed for others. Please write and share your beliefs with myself and others.

Melissa K. Larsen

mlarsen@ipa.net

Blessings to All

In a world where so many begin to say *why* to Christmas, there was a little girl who desperately wants to believe. Her life was changing as she knew it. Her parents were worried more, and she heard them talk in quiet voices. They were worried about what Christmas would be like this year. She listened to all they had to say and got more worried herself. Change has been so hard this year. The family had moved out of their fancy house into a much smaller one, miles away, where her father's new job is. She couldn't help but worry if the man in the red suit would find them. Why couldn't everything stay the same?

At her new school, she kept hearing the kids say that their parents weren't spending money on gifts this year. They were also saying the man in the red suit wasn't real and that he was causing many problems. Why would anyone want to carry on these silly traditions?

This puzzled Tabby Mae. Christmas had always been very special for her and her family. One of the things she loved most was going to the mall and sitting on the lap of the man in the red suit to tell him what she wished for. Then on Christmas morning, after church, the presents were always there. This was a joyful time for the family, and one that Tabby Mae would always say a prayer of thanks for.

Tabby Mae wondered, could it be true? Was there no truth to the man in the red suit? Why would anyone continue to spread this nonsense? Are you supposed to be a certain age, just to be told it wasn't true? Is it only for the young to share?

She went to her mom and dad and asked them, "Is the man in the red suit for real? Will he come this year?"

Her parents looked sadly at each other and really didn't know what to say. They replied more to each other than to Tabby Mae, "Should we tell her?"

Her mom looked worried and said "Why don't I take her and Chris to the mall Saturday, and she can ask the man in the red suit." Her father agreed. So Tabby Mae, her mom, and her little brother Chris were set to go to the mall the next day.

The entire way to the mall Tabby Mae wanted to ask her mother about the man in the red suit. She just couldn't, in front of Chris. He was so excited to see the man in the red suit. Could Tabby Mae dare get as excited as her little brother?

While waiting in line, she looked around and saw all the happy faces of children. She also heard the voices among the adults saying, "How are we going to afford presents? We don't have the money to get the presents they want. Maybe we should tell them the truth." This upset Tabby Mae because she could sense the stress and worry from the adults.

When it was her and Chris's turn, Chris eagerly went forward and Tabby Mae hung back. She just couldn't go up there. Right before her eyes, as she looked closely at the man in the red suit, he looked like any other man. Tabby Mae turned to her mother and said, "I'm too old for this. I will wait right here for you and Chris."

Her mom looked as sad as Tabby Mae felt, and asked, "Are you sure?"

"Yes mom, I'm sure," said Tabby Mae.

Her mom sighed and said quietly, "I guess you are getting older."

As Chris sat on the lap of the man in the red suit, he looked so happy. Sadness washed over Tabby Mae. She wanted to be as happy as her little brother. She wanted to dare to believe in all the wonderful feelings Christmas brings.

Tabby Mae stared more closely at the man in the red suit. He looked like he knew what she was feeling. There was a sparkle and a kindness and...wait! He was winking at her! Why was he doing this?

He motioned for her to come over to where he and Chris were. All the worry inside her wouldn't let her take the steps forward. The man in the red suit looked at her with such love. He reached out his hand and using his finger signaled for her to come. Chris seemed so happy and the man in the red suit looked so welcoming, could she take the steps forward?

A small, still voice inside her wanted so much to go and to believe in this man in the red suit. Poor Tabby Mae couldn't get past the voices of her parents, her friends at school, and even the adults she had heard in line. Sadness washed over her. Even though she really wanted to go, she refused. She just walked away.

Tabby Mae upsettingly asked, "Mom, did I do the right thing? Is the man in the red suit for real?"

"Tabby Mae, you need to wait until your father comes home. Then we both will talk to you. Let's not have this discussion in front of your little brother," her mother replied wearily.

Just then Tabby Mae felt a tug on her dress. Chris stared at his big sister puzzled. He asked, "Tabby Mae why didn't you go sit with me on the man in the red suits lap? Now is he supposed to know what you want for Christmas? He knows what I want!!!"

This did nothing to help Tabby Mae and suddenly the thought of growing up just wasn't as fun. She felt a heavy weight on her shoulders. She didn't know if she really wanted to have that talk with mom and dad. Plus mom didn't seem like she knew what to say and Chris was so excited.

Tabby Mae thought to herself "Is this what Christmas is like when you grow up? Are you supposed to worry about money and miss out on all the happiness? Do you dare to believe? What happens to the wonderful feelings of Christmas?"

All through the day and into the night Tabby Mae waited for her Dad to come home but it seemed like faith was going to keep her father away. He had taken a second job for the Christmas season. Tabby Mae wondered if the job had something to do with the man in the red suit. Is he the reason her parents were so sad and her dad wasn't home much? Was this the reason her mom hadn't bought any new decorations or even talked about the Christmas Eve party they always have? Was the party off? She wondered if there was any way she could help out this Christmas. If this would make her parents happier, Tabby Mae knew she wanted to help.

It got later and later and her dad still wasn't home.

"Tabby Mae, Chris is already in bed and you need to go to bed" quietly said her mom.

"Why?" Tabby Mae replied, "You said I could talk to you and dad."

"I know, but it is late. Be a good girl and go to bed as I asked you to." Her mom said, "Please! Let us say our prayers together."

Tabby Mae and her mom said their prayers and then it was lights out.

But the light wasn't turned off in Tabby Mae's head. She laid there wondering is he real, or not? What if? What is?

Cabby Mae heard her dad come in and decided to get up and talk to her parents. She quietly walked towards the living room and stopped. Peaking around the corner, she heard her parents talking.

Her mom was telling her dad about the mall and how Cabby Mae wouldn't go see the man in the red suit and how she wanted to talk to them. She could feel the tension and the worry. Dad looked sad and then to Cabby Mae's surprise she heard her mom say, "Maybe Cabby Mae is old enough to know the truth. Maybe we should tell her."

Dad answered her in a sharp tone, "I am working double time so this doesn't have to happen. I am not going to be the one to tell her. You should have bought more decorations and asked her to help you plan for the Christmas Eve party, like you've done every year. If we could only do all the things we used to be able to do, we wouldn't have to tell her anything. If you want to know why Cabby Mae is so upset, look around, we haven't done half the traditions we used to do!"

Mom's voice sounded so sad "I know, but I have been trying to save all the money I can to put towards the gifts. It has been so hard this year!"

Cabby Mae watched her dad rub his forehead, "Maybe we should focus on the true meaning of Christmas. The Christmas baking, the decorations, and cut back to only a few memorable gifts."

Mom sadly replied, "Then we will really have to talk to her."

Cabby Mae quickly and quietly ran back to her room before either of her parents saw her.

She kneeled down beside her bed and folded her hands in prayer.

"Dear God, I am sorry that I asked mom and dad about the man in the red suit. Please help them to be happy and allow our family to have the best Christmas, whatever that may be."

Tabby Mae decided to go to bed, not knowing just how powerful her prayer would be. She tucked herself into bed and closed her eyes, trusting God had heard her.

Tabby Mae didn't know how long she had been sleeping, when she felt a feather-light kiss across her cheek. She awoke. There, in her room, was the most beautiful angel. She had sparkling wings and all. She again kissed Tabby Mae's cheek and smiled at her.

Tabby Mae looked on in awe, wondering if this angel was the answer to her prayers. "Should I be scared," she asked herself. Yet to her amazement she wasn't scared. She was extremely peaceful and happy. The beautiful angel reached out her wings and spoke, "You asked God to show you if the man in the red suit is real. Do you dare to believe now?"

Eagerly Tabby Mae exclaimed, "Yes! Oh Yes!"

Lovingly the angel asked Tabby Mae, "Look around you." As Tabby Mae was looking on a huge, beautiful, white-light filled the room. Tabby Mae could see herself and the angel walking in a beautiful valley where everything was covered in shimmering white snow.

The angel touched Tabby Mae's cheek and asked her, "You love playing in the snow, don't you?"

"Oh, Yes!" answered Tabby Mae.

"Do you believe in making and in the power of snow angels?" the angel asked.

Tabby Mae looked up at her and questioned, "How do you know that?"

The angel peered down at Tabby Mae and said, "All the fun and wonderful memories are stored in your heart as you grow up. They can be reclaimed and you can think of them whenever you want," the beautiful angel said lovingly.

Tabby Mae loved all that was going on, but she had to ask the beautiful angel, "What does this have to do with the man in the red suit?"

"Well," said the beautiful angel, "sometimes you have to revisit your memories and connect with them before you can dare to believe."

The angel asked Tabby Mae to close her eyes and picture her favorite family traditions and decorations. Tabby Mae started to describe them, but could not describe them as fast as the beautiful angel was recreating them. The angel spread her wings. This created a sound that startled Tabby Mae. She peeked through her fingers and could not believe what she saw. As the angel's wings were fanning across her bed, a powerful light was created. Throughout the entire room appeared Tabby Mae's most treasured memories.

Since she knew Tabby Mae was peeking through her fingers, she lovingly asked, "What do you see?"

Tabby Mae couldn't believe the transformation her room had taken. There, right before her eyes, were all the images of Tabby Mae's favorite Christmas memories. There were also some images of people that she didn't recognize. She asked the Angel, "I know these memories, but who are these people?"

The angel only smiled and said, "These are memories yet to come."

Tabby Mae smiled back and gazed at all the beautiful sights. There were bright scenes of snowmen, angels, penguins, and presents. There were smiling happy faces and the smell of Christmas cookies and Christmas dinner. Music was playing, and in the middle of the scene was the man in the red suit.

Tabby Mae kept smiling, but she still didn't quite understand everything. She turned and asked, "Beautiful angel, what am I missing?"

The beautiful angel spread her wings, wrapped them around Tabby Mae, hugging her closely. Tabby Mae was asked by the angel to think about the man in the red suit, cover her heart with her hand, and tell her what she was feeling and seeing.

Tabby Mae didn't hesitate. She covered her heart with her hand. Slowly, she could see the man in the red suit changing.

Tabby Mae yelled out, "He is changing!"

The angel replied, "Just keep on believing."

All of a sudden Tabby Mae could feel the love radiate out of her heart and into the room. Once again the white-light illuminated the room with the images she was feeling. To her surprise, she could see the man in the red suit in front of a barn. He was kneeling down with a beautiful smile on his face.

Tabby Mae looked closer and she could see inside the barn. Inside was a beautiful baby wrapped in a cloth. The baby was surrounded by his mom and dad. She could feel the love, happiness, and wonder of it all.

Then she heard the prayer of the man in the red suit:

*"Father, I kneel beside you. Just a man in a red suit who started loving you the moment I felt you in my heart. I would see those who needed a reminder of the powerful gifts you give us each year through your birthday. So, I put on this red suit, go out and wrap small presents, and give them from my heart. It doesn't matter if they cost a little or a lot, it is only a reminder of the greatest gift we can ever give or receive. You, wrapped in this cloth, beginning a path to Easter, where you will give us true life. Forgive me Father, for I may have lead too many to forget what you had me really start. It saddens me to know there are those who think of the time, expense, work and stress of the season. When they really should be thinking of the messages they can give and receive. They do not know that this red suit represents your love and your life, which will always bring them true happiness and joy. I now accept and give these gifts to you, Father."*

Tabby Mae looked closer and the man in the red suit was presenting the Child with gifts. As the boxes were opened, each box was empty, except for the wonderful feeling you could feel. She looked even closer and touched her hand to her heart and asked the beautiful angel, "What am I to feel?"

The angel replied, "Just believe, and see what comes to you. Touch your heart."

Tabby Mae did as she was told. Then she saw herself with gifts to give and receive. She saw a gift of Hope, a gift of Peace, a gift of Faith, a gift of Joy, a gift of Comfort, a gift of Love, and a gift of Knowledge.

The angel spoke softly to Tabby Mae, "You are old enough to know the truth of the man in the red suit. He is a man who believes in the true gifts of Christmas. His name is St. Nick and he asks all of us to help him give the gifts the precious baby Child gives us each year. Christmas is a time for giving and receiving these gifts. Do you understand? It is just as important to be willing to receive and accept them, as it is to give them. It prepares you for your journey towards Easter."

Tabby Mae understood all too well and asked the angel to give her a hug.

The angel said, "Yes, this will please me." Tabby Mae reached out to hug the angel and felt the angel's wings wrap around her. It felt like her arms were long enough to wrap around them both.

Tabby Mae was startled when she realized she was hugging herself. Then she covered her heart with her hand and waited, until she felt the love and saw the images once again fill her room. She could see Christmas and what it means to all who dare to believe in the man in the red suit, and the seven gifts you get to give and receive.

Cabby Mae went to sleep knowing she had things to do in the next day. As soon as morning came, Cabby Mae jumped out of bed, touching her heart, with a huge smile in place. She ran to her parents' room as fast as she could.

"Mom, Dad I believe in the man in the red suit. I need to go to see him after church. Please, Please!"

Both parents were amazed and couldn't wait to take Cabby Mae to the mall.

Tabby Mae eagerly went to the mall and waited patiently for her turn to see the man in the red suit. She sat on his lap. He winked at her and she winked back.

The man in the red suit said, "Tabby Mae, what gifts would you like to receive this Christmas? "

Tabby Mae touched her heart with her hand, without questioning how he knew her name. She even knew what he wanted her to say.

Tabby Mae spoke up in a bright, loud voice for everyone to hear, "I am old enough to know I believe in the man in the red suit. I am here to tell you, I will give as well as receive the gifts of Christmas. What I want is for everyone to wrap up in a box and give the true gifts of Christmas; the gifts of Faith, Hope, Joy, Peace, Comfort, Love and Knowledge." She kissed the man in the red suit on the cheek and said, "Thank you for teaching us the true meaning of giving and receiving each year. "

Tabby Mae shouted out to her parents, "Mom, Dad, I love you! Can we give everyone we love and know these gifts? Let's not keep them to ourselves, but share them with all. Can we wrap up empty boxes as presents with these messages inside? Can we?" Tabby Mae and the man in red suit hugged each other and smiled. For they believe.

Her parents and others wiped away the tears, because all of a sudden they had been touched by one little girl and the man in the red suit. This man in the red suit did represent the gifts they received and were supposed to be giving each Christmas. At that moment, it didn't matter the size of the gift or the amount it cost. All it meant was sharing the story. A story which can be told and given each and every Christmas.

Tabby Mae and the man in the red suit leave you with just one question...Do <u>you</u> Dare to Believe?

# The End

# ABOUT THE AUTHOR

As a child, Melissa K. Larsen had avid interest in reading books, much more than interest in school. She was more likely to be found outside the school, or even under the dining room table, with a book. At one point, for a principal to keep her in school, she garnered herself a location in the library, where her class lessons were brought to her. The main stipulation was complete access to any book, and of course colas and crackers.

As a teen, a car accident left her with spinal cord damage. Melissa was told she would not improve and be in a wheel chair within 15 months. She looked at the Doctors and said; "Who are you, God??? I will beat this" and she did with His help. Her perseverance and persuasiveness continued as young adult; overseeing 100's of employees, training, arranging contracts, consulting and overseeing, helping them achieve their goals.

Unfortunately, she experienced several other damaging accidents, none of which were her fault. She moved on from her career, but never slowed down her reading interest.

The main thing that she never slowed down with, was the undying, unconditional love and guidance of her mother Edna Mae. She always kept Melissa focused on God and how each day is an unfolding miracle, if only you look at it. There are people to touch and be touched by, in an inspirational way, each and every day.

Melissa currently resides in Arkansas with her husband, yorkies and cats.

Printed in the United States
By Bookmasters